Coyotes

NORTHWORD
Minnetonka, Minnesota

DEDICATION
To Sarah, who has wild music in her heart.
–J.V.
ACKNOWLEDGEMENTS:
Thank you to wildlife biologist Eric Gese, Ph.D., for sharing his expert knowledge of coyotes.

© NorthWord Books for Young Readers, 2007

Photographs © 2007 provided by:
Photodisc/Punchstock: cover; Sumio Harada/Minden Pictures: back cover, pp. 10, 11, 31, 38, 45; Tom Vezo/Minden Pictures: pp. 4, 13; Michael Quinton/Minden Pictures: pp. 5, 14-15, 21, 23, 24; Konrad Wothe/Minden Pictures: pp. 8-9, 39; Tim Fitzharris/Minden Pictures: p. 12; Steven Tulissi/istockphoto: pp. 16-17; National Geographic Image Collection/Punchstock: p. 18; Mark Raycroft/Minden Pictures: p. 20; Creatas Images/Punchstock: pp. 28-29; John Flannery/Bruce Coleman Inc.: p. 32; Corbis/Punchstock: p. 36; Michael Durham/Minden Pictures: p. 37; istockphoto: p. 41; John Ray Upchurch/Shutterstock: p. 42.

Illustrations by Andrew Recher
Designed by Laurie Fritsche
Edited by Kristen McCurry

NorthWord Books for Young Readers
11571 K-Tel Drive
Minnetonka, MN 55343
1-888-255-9989
www.tnkidsbooks.com

Library of Congress Cataloging-in-Publication Data

Vogel, Julia.
        Coyotes / by Julia Vogel ; illustrations by Andrew Recher.
            p. cm. – (Our wild world)
        Includes index.
        ISBN: 978-1-55971-982-7 (hc) – ISBN: 978-1-55971-983-4 (sc)
        1. Coyotes—Juvenile literature. I. Recher, Andrew, ill. II. Title.

QL737.C22D86 2007
599.77'25--dc22
                                                2006101493

Printed in Singapore

10 9 8 7 6 5 4 3 2 1

OUR WILD™ WORLD SERIES

Coyotes

Julia Vogel
Illustrations by Andrew Recher

NorthWord
Minnetonka, Minnesota

JUST AFTER SUNSET, a pack of coyotes gathers on a hill and lift their noses toward the moon. *Yip, Yip, Yip! Ay-ee, Ay-ee! Howooo!* The coyotes' shrill cries fill the night.

To most people, a coyote's howl is a song of the Wild West. The eerie sound makes them picture tumbleweeds and cowboys around a campfire. But these days, you may hear coyotes in Connecticut as well as Arizona. They live through much of North America, from Canada to Mexico, and south to Panama. At a time when many other wild animal populations are shrinking, coyotes are spreading fast and far.

Why are they so successful? In Native American stories, Coyote is a crafty Trickster who often changes how he looks or acts to fool others. Scientists say coyotes are adaptable, which means they can change how they behave in different times and places. Adaptability is a big reason why coyotes now howl in every U.S. state except Hawaii.

Keen senses and sharp intelligence have helped coyotes spread through North and Central America.

Coyotes may howl alone or in groups to communicate with other coyotes.

Like timber wolves, foxes, and the family dog, coyotes belong to an animal family called *Canidae* (KAY-ni-dee). All canids are mammals, warm-blooded animals that have fur and nurse their young. The oldest canid fossils found so far are more than 50 million years old. Even those ancient coyote ancestors had the teeth of hunters. Long canid teeth called canines (KAY-nines) pierce the skin and hold prey. Carnassial (kar-NASS-ee-ul) teeth can slice meat and crush the bones of a coyote's dinner.

Coyotes are just one of 34 kinds, or species (SPEE-sees), of canids around the world. Coyote kin include Africa's tiny fennec fox, which weighs only 2 pounds (0.91 kg) and the widespread gray wolf, which may weigh a hefty 110 pounds (50 kg). Coyotes vary in size, too. In harsh desert environments, coyotes tend to be small, weighing about 20 pounds (9.1 kg), while coyotes living east of the Mississippi River may weigh more than 50 pounds (22.7 kg). Differences in size and other traits make scientists think there may be 19 different subspecies, or different kinds within the species. But all coyotes are given the same scientific name, *Canis latrans*, which is Latin for "barking dog."

Coyotes
FUNFACT:

Dogs and coyotes are so closely related that they sometimes mate. The offspring are called coydogs (KOY-dogs).

Coyote

Red Fox

Gray Wolf

Coyotes usually run with their bushy tails held low and straight.

Coyotes are also known by many other names. They are "God's dog" among Navajo people, while some Crow stories call them "Old Man Coyote." Early settlers from Europe named the animals prairie wolves. Other labels include brush wolves, burrowing dogs, song dogs, and American jackal. The English word coyote comes from the ancient Aztec word, *coyotl*. People even disagree about how to pronounce the animals' most familiar name. Are they *KY-oats* or *Ky-OH-tees*?

Coyotes
FUNFACT:

Coyote tracks show that their hind feet land in the same spots as their front feet when they're walking, a trait called "perfect walking."

A hunting coyote can leap far to pounce on its prey.

No matter what they are called, coyotes share traits that help them survive. Often mistaken for wolves, coyotes have pointier ears and longer, narrower snouts. Both species have bushy tails, but wolves may run with their tails curved and higher than their backs. Coyotes hold their tails straight out, below back-level. About 20 to 24 inches (51 to 61 cm) tall at the shoulder, coyotes are shorter as well as lighter weight than wolves. They have long legs, though, that make some think coyotes look like foxes on stilts.

Those slim, muscular legs are built for speed. Coyotes, like all canids, walk, trot, and run on their toes. Tough claws grip the ground and paw pads absorb shocks when they run and jump. During sharp turns, their bushy tails act like rudders to help them stay balanced. A healthy coyote can run almost 40 miles (64 km) per hour for short distances and spring 12 feet (3.7 m) into the air. They can even climb high fences and swim by dog paddling.

A thick fur coat protects coyotes from all kinds of weather. Long, coarse guard hairs shed rain and snow, while a soft, woolly undercoat insulates against cold winds. In bitter weather, they can curl into a circle, wrapped in the warmth of their black-tipped tails.

Thick fur helps this coyote sleep through a Rocky Mountain snowstorm.

These coyote tracks were probably made at night. By day, desert coyotes usually rest in the shade.

Adaptable coyotes can also stay cool in warm climates. Each spring, they shed much of their thick coat. Desert coyotes know to stay out of the sun, resting under a shady rock ledge by day and hunting at night. Like dogs, coyotes have few sweat glands in their skin and must pant to lose extra heat through their mouths and throats.

Coat colors vary from yellowish brown to reddish gray. Black-tipped hair often gives the animals a grizzled look. Most coyotes are darker on their backs, with cream-colored throats and bellies. Desert coyotes may be paler than coyotes living in northern states and Canada, but in the far north, coyotes may grow lighter-colored fur coats in winter for camouflage (KAM-uh-flaj) in the snow.

When Europeans first arrived in North America, coyotes lived in the southwestern deserts and central plains. As settlers cleared forests and planted fields in the 1800s, the animals learned to find mice, chickens, and other food around farms and ranches. As people spread west and north, coyotes followed.

Coyotes
FUNFACT:

Coyotes are true native wildlife. Their ancient ancestors, known only from fossils, lived in North America.

Desert coyotes often have paler fur than coyotes in other habitats. No matter where they live, coyotes need water to drink.

Snow can make finding and catching prey more difficult, but this coyote looks healthy and well fed.

Wolves still kept coyotes out of some areas by competing for prey and killing coyote pups. But wolves were hunted and trapped nearly to extinction in the early 1900s. People killed coyotes, too, blaming them for killing livestock just like wolves. Yet coyote numbers kept growing, and they moved in all directions. As they spread, the animals adapted to living in almost all kinds of habitats, including northern forests, rain forests, suburbs, and even cities.

Coyotes
FUNFACT:

Country coyotes may be active day or night, but city coyotes are mostly active at night to stay out of people's sight and out of daytime traffic.

Wolves once kept coyotes out of northern forests like the snowy woods this coyote calls home.

Eastern coyotes often look bigger and more wolf-like than western coyotes.
They also hunt deer and other large prey more often.

At first, people doubted that coyotes had reached the East Coast. How could western wildlife move so far from home? Besides, the animals glimpsed in eastern forests looked larger and heavier than grassland coyotes. Some believed the creatures were wolves, or maybe a hybrid, or mixed, animal that was part wolf and part coyote or part coyote and part dog. Coyotes, wolves, and dogs are so closely related that they can mate and have pups. Careful measurements of the mystery animals' skulls showed that they were most similar to coyotes. But later studies of their genetics, or inherited background, found that eastern coyotes have some gray wolf ancestors, too.

In the 21st century, coyotes are still expanding their range, the area where they live. In 2004, the first coyotes were spotted in the U.S. capital, Washington, D.C. Researchers in Boston, Chicago, and other cities and suburbs are counting more coyotes than they ever expected. Lack of water keeps them out of the driest deserts, but elsewhere they are often the most common large predator around. Wary of humans, coyotes rarely let people watch them for long. But listen for un-doglike yips, barks, and howls at night to learn if you, too, live in coyote country.

Coyotes
FUNFACT:

By howling, coyotes can send messages to other coyotes at least 0.62 miles (1 km) away.

Sharp eyes, ears, and nose can help a coyote find mice, grasshoppers, berries, and other food in a grassy meadow.

Whether ravens or coyotes find a dead animal first, the carcass makes a much-needed winter meal.

Wherever they live, coyotes rely on keen senses to survive. Although famous for night howling, they can be active both day and night. Their yellow eyes work well in bright light or darkness. By day, coyotes probably do not see colors as well as humans. But they are better than we are at spotting movement, such as a running deer or a hopping rabbit. Scientists think that eyesight is their most important sense for hunting.

Coyotes also have an unusual way to find food in daylight: by looking up. If ravens are circling in the sky, coyotes know that the birds may have found a dead deer or other carrion (KARE-ee-un) to eat. The canids will head for the place the ravens are circling, and, whether the birds like it or not, share their feast.

Like cats and some other night-active animals, coyotes have a special eye structure that helps them see better in the dark. The tapetum lucidum (tah-PEE-tum LEW-si-dum) works like a mirror, keeping more light inside the animals' eyes when they need it most. If your flashlight catches a coyote's face at night, the emerald green eyeshine you see comes from the tapetum lucidum.

Day and night, coyotes also use their eyes to get along with each other. They are social animals, often living in groups called packs. A coyote pack is typically made up of two parents and their offspring, from two to twelve animals. Living with all of those relatives, coyotes need to get along. They learn to recognize each other by sight and to use face and body signals that show their moods and feelings. Coyotes wag their tails in friendly greetings or flatten their ears and bare their teeth to warn others away. The signals are so important to coyote communication that researchers have named many of them. For example, in a "play dance," a coyote wags its tail and moves side-to-side to signal that it wants some fun.

Ears also help coyotes communicate and find food. Often, prey animals hide in burrows or under the snow. A hunting coyote will sometimes freeze, then tilt its head and turn its ears this way and that, picking up sounds from every direction. It may stand for several minutes, then suddenly leap into the air and land with all four feet on a mouse. The coyote's sharp hearing found the rodent even when its eyes couldn't see it.

Mice dig tunnels under the snow. Coyotes listen for their scratchings, then they punch through the snow to catch them.

This coyote snarls to defend a deer carcass he's eating.

Coyotes also use their ears to listen to each other. Some people think that coyotes are howling at the moon. You may sometimes hear their howls on moonlit nights, but they're not howling at the moon. They're communicating with each other. Sometimes, the piercing cries may be greetings to other family members. Other howls may be warnings to strange coyotes, meaning "Stay away!" Sometimes, scientists think that packs may get together and howl just for fun.

Coyotes make many other sounds to communicate. Several different sounds, including barks, growls, and teeth snaps, warn others when a coyote is angry or defending a kill. A coyote may also cry "Yi-e-e-e" if startled, whine softly if hurt or frightened, or call "Wow-Oo-Wow, Wow-Oo-Wow!" to greet others returning from a hunt. One unusual sound is huffing, made when a coyote snorts air out of its nose and mouth. A mother coyote may huff at her pups as a way to call them without making loud noises.

Noses also help coyotes communicate. Glands under each animal's tail make a pasty, musky liquid that other coyotes sniff during greetings. Every coyote in a pack knows the others by their unique smells. They also leave scent messages for each other along trails with urine or in piles of droppings, called scat. A coyote can even get clues about its family and neighbors by sniffing their tracks.

Coyotes
FUNFACT:

Coyote scat usually contains deer, mouse, or rabbit fur, plus crushed bones, seeds, and other leftover bits from their varied diets.

Scents also help coyotes communicate with coyotes they do not know. Each pack has a territory where it lives and hunts. Pack members will chase away or even fight with strangers that cross into their territory. To avoid such conflicts, pack members regularly visit the edges of their land. At special spots, such as bushes, trees, or rocks, the coyotes urinate and often scratch the ground. The smells and scratches at scent posts tell outsiders, "Keep out!"

Smells, sounds, and sights all alert coyotes to many different kinds of food.

They are predators, or animals that kill and eat other animals for food. But coyotes are also opportunists, meaning they take just about any opportunity for food that they can get. Depending on the season, their diet may include seeds, fruits, and vegetables, in addition to other animals. Ripe blueberries and persimmons attract coyotes in the woods, and apples or corn will bring them into a farmer's fields. In the Mojave Desert, they get some much-needed water from green gourds called coyote melons.

Coyotes
FUNFACT:

Like most canids, coyotes cannot pull in their claws. That means their claws are dull and not much use for killing prey, unlike cat claws.

Scavenging, or carrion-eating, also plays a big part in coyote diets. Elk killed by wolves, deer hit by cars, or cattle that died from disease all look tasty to hungry coyotes. In cities, talented scavengers find plenty to eat. A street-wise coyote knows just where to find open garbage cans, full dog food dishes, and leftover fast food for a midnight snack.

A coyote lucky enough to catch a big trout will defend it from foxes and other animals that might try to steal it.

Many kinds of prey animals also attract coyotes. Fawns, baby birds, and other newborn animals are easy targets in spring, while winter-starved adult deer become easier to catch late in the year. Other favorite wild prey includes mice, rabbits, and ground squirrels, plus grasshoppers and other large insects. Desert coyotes snatch up lizards and snakes, and coyotes living near streams catch frogs and fish. Alaskan coyotes gobble snowshoe hares. Farms and towns also provide plenty of hunting opportunities. Untended sheep, calves, chickens, and other livestock, as well as cats left alone outdoors may become coyote dinners.

Coyotes
FUNFACT:

Coyotes sometimes follow badgers while hunting. The badger digs down into a ground squirrel burrow, and the coyote catches the squirrel as it tries to escape.

How can coyotes hunt so many different animals? Unlike predators that specialize in one kind of prey, coyotes can change their hunting behavior. To catch small animals, coyotes usually hunt alone. A mouse-hunting coyote does not need help to stand and listen for scurrying in the grass. But catching a fast-moving jackrabbit may require teamwork. Two coyotes working together can take turns chasing a rabbit until it tires out. A whole pack may cooperate to catch large prey. A deer could outrun a lone coyote or defend itself with hooves and antlers. Chased by a pack, the deer's only escape may be to leap into deep water where coyotes rarely follow.

After a big kill, pack members often gorge, or eat as much as they can hold. They may not hunt again for several days. Packs do nearly all of their hunting within their own territories. That means territories with plenty of food can be smaller than territories with little to eat. In open country, territories may range in size from 5 to 50 square miles (13 to 130 sq km). Urban coyotes may have patchwork territories, made up of a yard here and a park there, connected by sidewalks, bridges, and other paths the animals use secretly at night.

Coyotes
FUNFACT:

Coyotes cannot predict when they will make a kill
or find food. When they can, they will eat
up to 15 pounds (6.8 kg) at one time in case
it is a long time until their next meal.

A pack works together to capture, kill, and defend the carcass of large prey.

Wherever they live, coyote packs usually have two leaders. They are called the alpha (AL-fuh) pair, the most powerful male and female in the group. The alphas lead when the pack attacks large prey, and they get to eat first. Other adults in the pack, called betas (BAY-tuhs), are usually grown offspring of the alphas. The family gets along well most of the time, hunting, resting, howling, and playing together.

Sometimes, play turns into a test of strength. Face-to-face, two coyotes bare their teeth, hunch their backs, and snarl. Is the alpha coyote still top dog? Such fights rarely turn bloody. A tough alpha

When challenged by another pack member, an alpha coyote will bare its sharp canine teeth. Such displays rarely turn into violent fights.

will stand its ground and snap its jaws, reminding the beta who is boss. Usually, the beta accepts defeat, rolling on its back or tucking its tail between its legs while scampering off. Only rarely will the alpha lose and run away, leaving its family forever.

An alpha pair stays together for years, sometimes for life. Season after season, they hunt and travel together throughout their territory. Sometime between January and March, the pair mates. The female starts looking for a place to have their pups, called a den.

She looks only in the central core of their territory, a 2 to 3 square mile (5.2 to 7.8 sq km) area near the center, where she feels very safe. Coyote packs sometimes let strangers pass through other parts of their territory, but they defend the core against all intruders.

A female may dig several new dens, perhaps one in a sandy slope and another under an old stump. Or, she may find a spot under a rocky ledge. More often, she looks for an old fox or badger den to shape for her family.

Coyotes
FUNFACT:

Dens are usually well hidden from view. But the opening often faces south so the pups have a sunny place to play outside.

Typically, a tunnel from 5 to 30 feet (1.5 to 9.2 m) long leads to a snug underground den. The female gradually adds other tunnels and entrances. After all that digging, coyotes may use the same den over and over. One coyote den in Yellowstone National Park has been used ever since it was discovered in 1940.

About 63 days after mating, the female crawls into the den to give birth. An average litter has six pups, but she may have as few as two or as many as twelve. Coyote litter sizes change, depending on how much food the parents can find. For example, in years when snowshoe hare numbers are booming, Alaskan coyotes have big litters, too. But in years when lots of predators are chasing few hares, coyotes have fewer young.

Newborn coyotes are blind, toothless, and unable to walk. They weigh just over half a pound (240 to 275 g), smaller than a brand-new German Shepherd puppy. They have short fur coats, but pups must snuggle close to their mom for warmth. For the first three weeks, they stay in the dark den, nursing and sleeping day and night.

Just as the pups depend on their mother, she depends on her mate. The female needs more food than ever to make rich milk for her hungry offspring, yet she cannot leave them to go hunting. Instead, the alpha male hunts for her. He may carry his catch home to her in his jaws. Or, he may return with a full stomach and cough up, or regurgitate (re-GUR-ji-tate), a meal of chipmunks or other prey that he swallowed whole. Whatever he brings, she eagerly gobbles it, then returns to the den.

The rest of the pack stays away from the den at first. Beta coyotes are curious about the new pups, who are their younger brothers and sisters. But they know the alpha female will chase them off if they come near. The family stays in touch often by howling back and forth.

The pups grow fast. Their eyes open and their teeth start to appear after about two weeks. By three weeks, they can walk well enough to stumble out of the den. Blinking their eyes in the sunshine, the pups meet their dad and big brothers and sisters for the first time. The adults sniff and lick the pups, getting to know their unique smells. The pups may beg for food by licking a grown-up's mouth. The adult then regurgitates partly chewed and digested food, soft enough for puppy teeth to munch.

The mom can now go hunt for herself. The pups stay close to the den, with other pack members babysitting. The sitters watch for mountain lions, badgers, and other predators that kill young coyotes. If a babysitter spots danger, he or she warns the pups with a "Woof!"

A hungry pup licks an adult's mouth, asking for a warm meal.

They dash back inside. If their mother still feels the pups are unsafe, she will move them to another den.

When her pups are about seven weeks old, the mother weans them, or stops nursing. Adult pack members still deliver food, and one day, a live mouse arrives. The pups tumble over each other, yipping and scrambling after their first prey. That first mouse may escape, but the pups have begun to learn important hunting skills.

Eventually, the adults will take them along on hunts, showing the pups where to look for food, when to listen for ground squirrels, and how to wait patiently until just the right moment to pounce. By watching adults, young coyotes quickly learn many things that help them survive.

At nine weeks of age, this pup may have stopped nursing. But it still depends on its family for food and protection.

Pups spend much of their first summer playing. Without squeaky balls and old slippers, the pups turn sticks, pinecones, and grasshoppers into toys. Adults put up with the youngsters climbing over their backs, nipping their ears, and pouncing on their tails. One favorite game is play-fighting. Pups growl at each other, tussle in the dirt, and play tug-of-war over scraps of meat. These friendly battles help pups grow strong and learn which one is the strongest of all.

Pups leave the den for good when they are about two to three months old. They join the rest of the pack in an area

Pups learn from each other how to get along with other coyotes.

Even sleepy adults try to be patient when pups climb on them, nip their ears, and pull their tails.

of the territory called the rendezvous (RAHN-day-voo), sleeping outdoors from then on. When night falls, their yips and yowls mix with adults' howls. The pack announces to the night that they are a family and this is their home.

By about nine months old, the pups look like adults. But most do not survive their first year. Diseases, accidents, starvation, and predators kill young coyotes. Only a coyote with good hunting skills, quick wits, and good luck will reach 10 years of age. In protected areas, the average coyote life span is about six to eight years.

Hunger problems increase in late fall as food gets harder to find. Often, the home territory does not have enough food for all of the pups to stay. Many young coyotes leave their homes in autumn. Lone coyotes, or loners, may wander 50 to 100 miles (80 to 160 km) from their packs, which is one major reason why coyotes have spread so far across the continent.

A loner lives on the edges of other packs' territories, struggling to stay alive. It lacks help for catching large prey and for fighting off wolves and other enemies. It even has trouble chasing off vultures to snatch a bite of carrion. But if it can find a mate, the loner's chances of survival improve. Then the new pair may find a territory and start a pack of its own.

Coyotes
FUNFACT:

Coyotes are the state animal in South Dakota. Farmers there value them for killing mice and other small creatures that might otherwise eat their crops.

Coyotes sometimes prey on calves and other livestock, but they also eat voles and other crop-damaging wildlife.

In winter, even coyotes that stay with their parents may face hunger. Deep snows make mice hard to reach and deer hard to chase. In cities, starving coyotes dig into garbage dumps and raid backyard bird feeders. In wilderness, carrion of winter-killed bison or other large prey may be the only thing that saves the pack.

Cars endanger coyotes even in places that protect wildlife such as Wyoming's Grand Teton National Park.

Year round, the greatest threats to coyotes come from humans. Cars hit thousands every year, and still more are shot or poisoned to protect sheep and other livestock. Some are trapped for their fur coats or because city residents fear coyotes will spread disease or attack pets or children. Though people rarely see coyotes, some do not like having them around. Such attitudes toward coyotes are the biggest problem the animals face.

Yet even when people try to reduce coyote numbers, they keep spreading. Amazingly, if coyotes are being killed, they can reproduce more quickly. Alpha females in a pack may have larger litters, and beta females may give birth, too. Usually, coyotes do not mate until they are at least two years old. But when a coyote population is shrinking, young males and females may pair up and have pups when just one year old. The ability to change how fast they reproduce is another adaptation helping coyotes succeed.

How can people solve their problems with coyotes? Research has shown that farmers can protect their sheep from coyotes by keeping dogs, donkeys, or even llamas near the flock. Other scientists are playing recordings of coyote howls outdoors, testing to see if just the sounds of a pack make wild packs stay away. City residents have learned that covering trash cans, feeding dogs indoors, and keeping cats inside will help keep coyotes out of their yards.

Perhaps most important, people are learning to value coyotes. By eating mice, voles, and prairie dogs, coyotes protect farm crops. Some kinds of wildlife also benefit from having coyotes around. For example, ravens once scavenged off wolf kills in some areas, but their populations fell when wolves disappeared. Where coyotes move into old wolf territory, ravens may also make a comeback by feeding on coyote kills. Understanding that coyotes are part of the natural world helps people learn to live with them.

Coyotes are a wildlife success story. More coyotes are living in more places than ever before. Chances are, some live not far from you. Keep your ears open for their howling cries. That sound is the voice of a remarkable, adaptable animal, a reminder that we share our world with wildlife.

This female is taking a ground squirrel to her pups, the next generation of wild coyotes.

Internet Sites

You can find out more interesting information about coyotes and lots of other wildlife by visiting these Internet sites.

Animal Diversity Web
http://animaldiversity.ummz.umich.edu/site/accounts/information/Canis_latrans.html

California Department of Fish and Game
www.dfg.ca.gov/keepmewild/coyote.html

Desert USA
www.desertusa.com:80/june96/du_cycot.html

Environmental Education for Kids
www.dnr.state.wi.us/org/caer/ce/eek/critter/mammal/coyote.htm

The Humane Society
www.hsus.org/wildlife/a_closer_look_at_wildlife/coyote.html

National Geographic for Kids
www.nationalgeographic.com/kids/creature_feature/0005/coyote.html

Nature Park.com (coyote sound byte)
www.naturepark.com/coyinfo.htm

New York State Department of Environmental Conversation
www.dec.state.ny.us/website/dfwmr/wildlife/coyinny.htm

Smithsonian National Zoological Park
http://nationalzoo.si.edu/Publications/ZooGoer/2005/4/coyotes.cfm

Stanley Park Ecology Society (quiz)
www.stanleyparkecology.ca/programs/activities/coyoteQuiz.php

Washington Department of Fish and Wildlife
http://wdfw.wa.gov/wlm/diversity/living/coyotes.htm

Index

Titles available in the Our Wild World Series:

ALLIGATORS AND CROCODILES
ISBN 978-1-55971-859-2

BATS
ISBN 978-1-55971-969-8

BISON
ISBN 978-1-55971-775-5

BLACK BEARS
ISBN 978-1-55971-742-7

BUTTERFLIES
ISBN 978-1-55971-967-4

CARIBOU
ISBN 978-1-55971-812-7

CHIMPANZEES
ISBN 978-1-55971-845-5

COUGARS
ISBN 978-1-55971-788-5

COYOTES
ISBN 978-1-55971-983-4

DOLPHINS
ISBN 978-1-55971-776-2

EAGLES
ISBN 978-1-55971-777-9

FALCONS
ISBN 978-1-55971-912-4

GORILLAS
ISBN 978-1-55971-843-1

HAWKS
ISBN 978-1-55971-886-8

LEOPARDS
ISBN 978-1-55971-796-0

LIONS
ISBN 978-1-55971-787-8

LIZARDS
ISBN 978-1-55971-857-8

MANATEES
ISBN 978-1-55971-778-6

MONKEYS
ISBN 978-1-55971-849-3

MOOSE
ISBN 978-1-55971-744-1

ORANGUTANS
ISBN 978-1-55971-847-9

OWLS
ISBN 978-1-55971-915-5

PENGUINS
ISBN 978-1-55971-810-3

POLAR BEARS
ISBN 978-1-55971-828-8

PRAIRIE DOGS
ISBN 978-1-55971-884-4

SEA TURTLES
ISBN 978-1-55971-746-5

SEALS
ISBN 978-1-55971-826-4

SHARKS
ISBN 978-1-55971-779-3

SNAKES
ISBN 978-1-55971-855-4

TIGERS
ISBN 978-1-55971-797-7

TURTLES
ISBN 978-1-55971-861-5

VULTURES
ISBN 978-1-55971-918-6

WHALES
ISBN 978-1-55971-780-9

WHITETAIL DEER
ISBN 978-1-55971-743-4

WILD HORSES
ISBN 978-1-55971-882-0

WOLVES
ISBN 978-1-55971-748-9

NORTHWORD
Minnetonka, Minnesota